Battered by last year's Brexit vote, the spread of Euroscepticism across the continent, and a string of bloody terrorist attacks, the champions of the European Union breathed a sigh of relief when, on October 24, Germany's Angela Merkel won a fourth term as Chancellor. Following the earlier defeats of nationalist parties in France, Austria, and the Netherlands, the challenges to the sixty-year-old union of European countries seemed to have been turned back, and Merkel's victory to have justified the optimism of the March 25 celebrations of the sixtieth anniversary of the Treaty of Rome, which began the process of what it called "an ever-closer union among the peoples of Europe." Sixty years later, the E.U. representatives talked of a "strong community of peace, freedom, democracy, human rights and the rule of law," and reaffirmed their commitment to an "undivided and indivisible" Union.

But the cheers for Merkel and bravado of the Eurocrats could not quiet the discontent and malaise that have long troubled this "bold, far-sighted" project.

Indeed, ominous signs attended Merkel's reelection. Votes for her coalition comprising the Christian Democratic Union and the Christian Social Union fell by eight percentage points, the worst showing since 1949. Even more shocking, the nationalist and anti-immigration Alternative for Germany (AfD) was the Banquo's ghost at the celebration, winning nearly 13% for a third-place finish, and bringing a nationalist party into Parliament for the first time in more than 50 years. Protests against AfD broke out across Germany, as the German left, emboldened by Merkel's need of the leftist Greens to form a governing coalition, had to be kept away from AfD celebrations by police, as protestors hurled bottles and shouted "Nazi pigs!" A likely splintered Parliament in Germany, the E.U.'s richest and most consequential member, shows that the fault lines long threatening the "ever-closer union" have not been repaired, but are deepening.

Those divisions among member states and peoples are nothing new, and fretting over the viability and inequities of the E.U. has been constant since its birth. A decade ago several books analyzed the various problems,

The Europeans themselves have also been chronically worried about the future of the E.U. almost from the day it was created in Rome sixty years ago.

especially Muslim immigration, confronting the E.U. – Bruce Bawer's *While Europe Slept*, Claire Berlinski's *Menace in Europe*, Melanie Phillip's *Londonistan*, Walter Laqueur's *The Last Days of Europe*, and my own *Decline and Fall: Europe's Slow-Motion Suicide* all identified the problems undermining the viability and solidarity of the E.U. Last year Douglas Murray's *The Strange Death of Europe* continued the autopsy in light of more recent events.

The Europeans themselves have also been chronically worried about the future of the E.U. almost from the day it was created in Rome sixty years ago. Such malaise also marked the fiftieth-anniversary celebrations. That event was "shadowed by a sense that the union is stuck in something like a midlife crisis – unhappy about its divided present, uncertain about what path to take in the future," according to the *New York Times*. Such doubt was reflected in polls that found less than half of Europeans approved of the E.U.

The 2008 financial crisis focused this discontent: Greece's near default on its sovereign debt and the continuing threat of a Grexit; the humiliation of accepting a multibillion-dollar International Monetary Fund contribution to the E.U.'s near-trillion-dollar bailout fund; the renewal of old nationalist differences and enmities between the North and South; and the still-simmering economic crises stalking states like Italy and France – all laid bare the economic inequities and disparities among the various E.U. states, and challenged the ideal of transnational unity and harmony. More recently, the Brexit vote and the influx of 1.3 million refugees just in 2015, the majority from war-torn Syria and Afghanistan, have further highlighted the contradictions and questionable assumptions of the transnational, technocratic idealism defining the "new Europe."

Decades of crises large and small are seemingly propelling the E.U. and Europe in general toward the point where the stresses become unsustainable and lead to dissolution or a reconfiguration of the Union. This "bold, far-sighted" experiment has been troubled from its birth, and the "European Dream," as one champion has called it, may be nearing its last days.

The E.U. Economy

Numerous critics of the E.U. have for years pointed out that its collective economy chronically underperforms because of an intrusive regulatory regime, high taxes, and expensive social welfare benefits. The data tell the tale. The E.U.'s GDP of $16.5 trillion is close to that of the U.S. at $18.4 trillion. But average per capita GDP in the E.U. is significantly lower: $35,634 compared to $57,468 in the U.S. Look more closely at individual E.U. member states, and stark inequalities emerge: Germany's $41,963 or Denmark's $53,417, more than double Greece's $18,104 or Hungary's $12,664 (the lowest U.S. state per capita GDP is Mississippi's $31,881). The same disparities exist for unemployment rates. The Eurozone rate is 9.3%, compared to 4.4% in the U.S. But rates in the E.U. range from Germany's 3.9% to Greece's 22.5%. For young people (under age 25) rates are worse: 21% for the Eurozone, with the same divisions between North and South: 7% in Germany versus 47.3% in Greece.

Regulatory excess, high businesses taxes, and generous social welfare spending also contribute to the E.U.'s economic malaise. On the World Bank's "ease of doing business" scale, with 1 awarded to economies that are the friendliest to business, the U.S. earns an 8, while the two largest economies in the E.U., Germany and France, rank 17 and 29 respectively. The E.U. as a whole ranks 30. High tax rates also are a drag on economic growth. The U.S. averages 30% of income in total taxes, the E.U. 45%. As for spending on social welfare programs, the U.S. and the E.U. both spend roughly 21% of GDP. This last statistic should remind us that the U.S. has been steadily eroding the economic advantages it enjoys over the E.U.

These economic disparities in part explain the divisiveness that erupted during the 2008 Great Recession, and the continuing resentment of the poorer E.U. countries against the richer like Germany, on whom they have had to rely for financial help. Such divisions are a powerful centrifugal force that challenges the solidarity of the E.U. member states, and give teeth to the charge that the E.U. has benefitted Germany and other rich countries more than Europe as a whole.

Unfortunately, there are few signs that the

E.U. is making significant changes to head off another fiscal calamity. The debt crisis afflicting Greece, which after three bailouts owes almost $390 billion it is unlikely to pay back, remains unresolved. More worrisome is the condition of France, the second-largest economy in the E.U. and sixth largest of the world's sovereign nations. Unemployment is nearly 10%, youth unemployment double that. Economic growth is one of the weakest in the Union: 1.3% compared to 1.7% for the Eurozone, 1.9% for the E.U., and 3.9% for Germany. Taxes on employees are the high-

---

Decades of crises are seemingly propelling the E.U. toward the point where the stresses become unsustainable and lead to dissolution or a reconfiguration of the Union.

---

est in the E.U.: nearly 58% of a salary's cost goes to the government. Public debt is expected to reach 96% of GDP in 2017, and government spending as a percentage of GDP ranks second among OECD countries, 56% compared to 38% in the U.S. Social welfare spending takes 30% of GDP, ten points higher than the U.S and the E.U. average.

The E.U. very likely can survive the economic crisis in Greece, but not one in France. As historian Walter Russell Mead writes, "The most likely outlook is for continuing economic and political stagnation in France, a few inadequate reforms that are bitterly resented and resisted, and a gradual, continuing rise in social tensions and alienations." If new French President Emmanuel Macron cannot deliver on significant economic reforms as he promised – a likely scenario given the serial failure of previous French leaders – the damage to the E.U. will be devastating.

* * *

Demography

Another bad sign for Europe's economic health is the failure of Europeans to reproduce. It takes an average of 2.1 children per woman just to replace a population; Europe's average is 1.55, and it's that high in part because of more fecund immigrants. Looking deeper into individual countries reveals numbers even more dismal. Italy's rate is 1.43, Spain's 1.49, Portugal 1.53, and Poland 1.34 – and those are traditionally Catholic countries. Economic powerhouse Germany's is 1.44.

This demographic decline, along with increasing longevity, means that all these countries will grow older and older, as schools close, playgrounds empty, and millions of people grow up without aunts, uncles, or cousins. Today the average age in the E.U. is 42.4 years, and by 2080 30% of Europeans will be 75 and older. These projections bode ill for the E.U.'s economic future. By 2060, on average Europe will have only two workers for every retiree, and 12% fewer people in the workforce. The E.U.'s richest country, Germany, whose working-age population will shrink from 50 million in 2008 to between 34 and 38 million in 2060, alone will need 1.5 million new workers to stabilize its retirement system.

Without growth in the workforce, old-age pensions and health care will eat up more and more of national wealth even as fewer workers are paying taxes, leading to economic stagnation and greater debt and deficits. Fewer productive people also mean less dynamism in the economy, for human creativity and entrepreneurial "animal spirits" are modern capitalism's greatest resources. The uneven effects of these trends across Europe will deepen the fault lines already running through the E.U. project.

The Democracy Deficit

Much of European resentment against the E.U. focuses on the so-called "democracy deficit." For all the rhetoric of an "ever-closer union" of the European peoples, the E.U. is more accurately a union not of peoples, but of national ministers and governments. The ordinary citizen has little say in what policies are adopted, and the bureaucrats running the Union are seldom accountable or even known to voters.

This concentration of unaccountable power is obvious in the ruling structure of the E.U. Member-state citizens vote directly only for the European Parliament, which votes on, but cannot initiate, legislation. The other three main governing bodies are responsible for legislating and executing laws. The European Council is made up of the heads of states from each member state, and they set the policy agenda for the Union. The Council of Ministers, one minister from each member state chosen by the topic under consideration, has legislative and executive power. Finally, the European Commission is the main executive branch of the government. It comprises political appointees from each member state, and is responsible for drafting and enforcing the laws of the E.U. Meanwhile, the European Court of Human Rights and the Court of Justice of the European Union can trump national laws and violate the rights of member states and their citizens.

This top-heavy structure, comprising mostly member-state government ministers and appointees, insulates the governing bodies from direct accountability to the people, and compromises the transparency democratic citizens need in order to monitor those who make decisions affecting their lives. This disdain for *vox populi* became obvious in 2005, when the Treaty Establishing a European Constitution was put before the voters in France, the Netherlands, and Ireland, and they rejected it. The 2009 Treaty of Lisbon that created the European Constitution did not risk the voters' disapproval, but was signed by representatives from each member state, and ratified by member-state governments, with the exception of Ireland, which did hold a referendum. Britain's successful popular referendum to leave the E.U. ensures that Brussels will not again make the mistake of consulting the will of the masses.

Equally significant is the hypocritical contradiction between the transnational ideals of a government supposedly able to transcend parochial, zero-sum national interests, and the privileging of government officials, ministers, and appointees from sovereign nations in deciding how the Union is managed. Such a structure guarantees that the national interests of each state will take precedence, and more powerful states like Germany and France will trump those of lesser states. The primacy of national interests became obvious during the 2008 economic crisis, and more recently the 2015 influx of refugees and migrants. But even before the E.U. violated Article 125 of the Lisbon Treaty, which prohibits financial bailouts, in order to rescue Greece, E.U. members had ignored the E.U.'s fiscal rules. The Stability and Growth Pact of 1998 put a 3% of GDP limit on budget deficits, and 60% limit on national

> *It takes an average of 2.1 children per woman just to replace a population; Europe's average is 1.55.*

debt. In subsequent years every country except three has at some point violated the 3% limit on deficits. As for the 60% limit on debt, in 2015 the average national debt was 83% for the E.U., and 90% for the Eurozone. George Washington's wisdom remains valid: "No nation can be trusted farther than it is bounded by its interests."

For all its rejection of nationalism and its centrifugal cultures, interests, and mores, the E.U. in practice bypasses the particular, diverse peoples of Europe, instead putting decision-making in the hands of political elites from sovereign nations, who often have more in common with their fellow elites than they do with their own citizens. And that means more powerful nations will benefit more from the E.U. than will the less powerful. This division accounts for much of the discontent with the E.U. on the part of those European nations like Greece, who feel pushed around by Germany; or like the East European nations lectured to by E.U. officials like Commission President Jean-Claude Juncker, who haughtily said of those opposing Angela Merkel's feckless immigration policy, "I would invite those in Europe who try to change the migration agenda we have adopted – I would like to remind them to be serious about this and not to give in to these base reactions that I do not like." As in Orwell's *Animal Farm*, some E.U. member states are more equal than others.

Muslim Immigration

The problem of immigration into Europe from developing nations, particularly Muslim ones, has bedeviled Europe long before the creation of the E.U. Migration to Europe accelerated in the decades after the Second

World War. Migrants came first as "temporary" workers, many from underdeveloped regions of their home countries – Turks to Germany, Pakistanis to England, Algerians to France. In the following years "asylum seekers" and "political refugees," many of them economic migrants in disguise, added to their numbers. E.U. and British laws forbid deporting migrants, even murderers, to any country where they might face the death penalty or harsh abuse, and lax "family reunification" protocols increase numbers even further.

These ill-conceived immigration policies have been abetted by leaders in many European countries who have seen immigration as the solution to the problem of low birth rates and the need for workers to pay the taxes necessary for financing generous social welfare benefits – "replacement populations," as the U.N. calls them, for the Europeans not being born. In Germany, Chancellor Angela Merkel's open invitation to migrants from the Middle East has been rationalized with this argument. Germany alone will need

500,000 immigrants per year through 2050, reports the Bertelsmann Foundation. "Immigrants are really important to fill the shortage of workers," and so "immigration helps Germany and is really good and useful," according to Axel Plünnecke, a professor at the Cologne Institute, which estimates that by 2020 Germany will need a million workers for jobs in science, technology, and engineering. Unfortunately, most immigrants come with few marketable skills needed by a modern economy, resist the necessary job training, and are eligible for welfare transfers, leaving them with little incentive to train for jobs.

More important, the E.U. has not made it easy for European countries to demand and enforce assimilation to the home country's culture, mores, and values. Many Muslim immigrants, living in an increasingly irreligious and hedonistic European culture inimical to the tenets of their faith, have found little incentive or inclination to assimilate to an "infidel" culture. Strict and lengthy citizenship requirements, and burdensome regulations on job hiring, at the same time that generous welfare transfers have been available to immigrants, have reinforced this faith-based preference for self-segregation.

The result has been immigrant enclaves walled off from the larger culture, from the *banlieues* of Paris to the satellite "dish cities" of Amsterdam, the Small Heath district of Birmingham to the Molenbeek neighborhood of Brussels, which England's *The Guardian* reports is "becoming known as Europe's jihadi central." It's no surprise that they congregate in these "no-go zones," areas police rarely enter or patrol, where they remain underemployed, undereducated, and overrepresented in prisons and on welfare rolls.

All these circumstances have made young Muslims ripe for self-radicalization or recruitment by jihadists, often through local mosques and Islamic centers. Even before the latest influx of migrants in 2015, various intensities of social disorder and creeping Islamization were growing, from sharia courts in England to Muslims in Paris taking over public spaces to perform daily prayers, to gangs of Muslim men in Berlin enforcing sharia law in the streets. Violent crimes have increased over the last several decades, a disproportionate number of them perpetrated by second- and third-generation and recent immigrants. In France, for years burning cars has been a chronic ritual of violence committed mainly by young Muslim men. A thousand cars were burned last New Year's Eve, and, on Bastille Day in 2017, riots in Muslim districts of Paris broke out and raged for two days, leaving nearly a thousand burned cars. Sweden averages one car burned a day, and is plagued by other acts of violence and vandalism, particularly during Ramadan. Riots over police actions, and gang attacks on trains, shops, and government buildings are also common, as are acid attacks against women, usually Muslim, deemed to be in violation of Islamic law.

This violent criminal disorder has been exacerbated by over a million male migrants allowed into Europe over the last few years, among whom are thousands of jihadists and veterans of the conflict in Syria. In Germany during the first five months of 2017, 1,600 attacks with knives, machetes, and axes, an average of ten per day, were reported. Over the last ten years, such crimes have increased 1,200%, from 300 in 2007 to about 4,000 in 2016. Honor killings have surged as well, as has genital mutilation of Muslim girls. That same year the number of immigrants suspected of criminal acts increased nearly 53%. Sweden is another European country that has enthusiastically welcomed immigrants, mostly from Muslim countries, going back to 1975. Since then, as of 2015, violent crime increased by 300%, and as of 2014, rape by 1,472%. In 2010, Sweden had the third-highest number of women raped per 100,000 in the world.

Indeed, across Europe a "rape jihad," as Andrew C. McCarthy calls it, is underway. In Denmark, between 2004 and 2010 one-third of those convicted of sexual assault were immigrants. In the northern English town of

Rotherham, gangs of mostly Pakistani immigrants for years were sexually preying on children and girls, at least 1,400 between 1997–2013. In Cologne, on New Year's Eve of 2015 nearly a thousand women were attacked and sexually assaulted by gangs of immigrant men. Other attacks took place in Hamburg and Stuttgart. Austria has been especially victimized by these brazen attacks, perpetrated mainly be Afghan refugees in public spaces like trains, parks, and swimming pools. In just one issue of *Österreich*, a free newspaper distributed daily on public transit, three attempted rapes by Afghan immigrants were reported.

These daily criminal acts, which Norwegian writer Fjordman calls the "Little Terror," rarely make it to the attention of the global media, unlike the deadly terrorist attacks that have increased over the last few years. Between 2014 and 2017, there have been over 150 attacks and plots. France was attacked 10 times (237 dead); Britain has suffered four attacks just in 2017 (35 dead), the most recent a bungled attempt against a London subway that left 26 wounded; Brussels was attacked four times (36 dead); Germany five times (12 dead); Sweden once (5 dead); Spain once (14 dead); and Denmark and Finland once (each attack leaving two dead). Over 1,400 have been injured in these attacks, a toll that exceeds the number killed in the spectacular public transit attacks in Madrid in 2004 (191 dead) and London in 2005 (52 dead). But in some ways they are more demoralizing, since a larger and greater variety of Europe's public spaces are being attacked more frequently, increasing people's fear and sense of vulnerability.

The ordinary citizen has little to say in what policies are adopted, and the bureaucrats running the Union are seldom accountable or even known to voters.

And given the tens of thousands of jihadi agents that have come to Europe in the last few years, such attacks are sure to continue in the future.

The E.U.'s response to these attacks, moreover, has put further strains on European unity. After the influx of 2015 and the dramatic increase in terror attacks, many countries, including Austria, Denmark, Germany, Norway, and Sweden, reimposed some border controls, a de facto revision of the Schengen Area agreement that allows free travel among all 27 E.U. states. In 2015 Eastern European states like Hungary, Poland, the Czech Republic, and Slovakia started building physical barriers on their borders, and refused to accept any refugees. In June 2017 the European Commission initiated disciplinary proceedings against Poland, Hungary, and the Czech Republic for refusing to accept their assigned quotas of migrants, even though the majority of those countries' citizens – 70% in Hungary – are against allowing Syrian migrants into their countries.

The charges of xenophobia, racism, and other "base reactions," as Jean-Claude Juncker said, from many Western European leaders; their seeming indifference to the social disorder, crime, and terrorism many migrants are bringing into Europe; and their arrogant insensitivity to the different cultural mores, religiosity, and histories of Eastern European countries, have all widened the fissures among E.U. member states.

Also divisive has been many European countries' bad habit of allowing Muslims and Islamic organizations to impose their religious beliefs and mores on the wider culture and public spaces. Christian churches in Europe are being demolished – 2,800 are slated for destruction in France alone – even as more and bigger mosques are being built, some financed by the Qataris, who fund radicals in Libya, Iraq, and Somalia. One of Christendom's great cathedrals, in Córdoba, is currently under attack by jihadist Muslims and left-wing Spanish secularists, who want to turn it into a "space for the meeting of faiths," virtually desacralizing it. Sharia courts – 100 just in London – are allowed to function, no matter how much they violate the host country's laws, particularly on matters of divorce, family life, and the treatment of women.

Such appeasement includes the violation of citizens' right to free and open speech. E.U. and government officials and institutions regularly censor their agencies and punish their citizens in order to avoid the charge of "racism" or "Islamophobia": ignoring illiberal and sexist sharia courts, and not prosecuting those who practice polygamy and forced marriages; pressuring social media networks like Facebook and Twitter to censor alleged "hate speech" posts and websites like Jihad Watch and the Gatestone Institute; convicting Dutch politician Geert Wilders of "insulting a group and inciting discrimination" for publicly demanding fewer Moroccan migrants to the Netherlands; attributing anti-Semitic violence to right-wing extremists rather than to Muslims who commit the lion's share of attacks; arresting a candidate for the European Parliament for reading aloud excerpts about Islam from Winston Churchill's *The River War*; suppressing the ethnic and religious identities of criminal suspects, as the Germans did after the New Year's Eve assaults in Cologne, and not making available public statistics on sexual crimes; prosecuting citizens for "hate speech" who publicly criticize migrants; banning sexually suggestive billboards and advising women to avoid miniskirts, bikinis, and other revealing clothing; and tolerating extremist mosques and *madrassas* like those in the Manchester area that teach jihadist martyrdom and anti-Semitism.

Cultural and educational institutions similarly bow to pressure from Islamic groups over art exhibits, museum shows, theatrical performances, and school curricula, dress codes, and cafeteria menus. So it is that Europeans censor themselves and violate Western canons of free and open speech and artistic expression. The Gatestone Institute's Giulio Meotti, for example, documents instances where organizers of exhibits with Muslim themes or images have caved in to protests from Islamic groups and shut down shows and exhibits: in Maastricht, birthplace of the E.U.; at the Tate Gallery and Victoria and Albert Museum in London; the Museum of World Culture in Sweden; the Hergé Museum in Louvain, Belgium, which had planned an exhibition paying tribute to the *Charlie Hebdo* cartoonists murdered in a jihadist terror attack; and a whole section of Paris' Louvre Museum dedicated to Eastern Christians, currently suffering a genocidal jihad in the Middle East.

Meanwhile, Paris is building a $20 million bulletproof glass wall around the Eiffel Tower to protect it from possible terrorist attacks, while German Chancellor Angela Merkel has declared that she will not put a limit on "refugees" granted asylum in Germany. This official appeasement and hypocrisy feeds the anger and resentment of ordinary Europeans, who for years have been living with the wages of allowing large, unvetted numbers of ethnically, religiously, and culturally different peoples to settle in Europe.

All these problems of Muslim immigration reflect more than just intercultural misunderstandings or a failure of assimilation. For modern jihadist theorists, immigration into Europe has long been an explicit tactic for a slow-motion jihadist conquest in "stages." Higher birth rates of Muslim immigrants have also been seen as a weapon for transforming Europe, where today the average Muslim woman is ten years younger, and has 2.1 children compared to Christians' 1.6. Moreover, in 2015, for the first time in modern history, the European population declined, with 5.1 million births compared to 5.2 million deaths. According to Pew Research Center, by 2050, Europe's population will have declined by 99.2 million, while the Muslim population will have increased by 27.4 million.

If these trends continue, they will fulfill the alleged prophecy of Algerian President Houari Boumediene, who in 1974 said, "One day millions of men will leave" the South for

The problem of immigration into Europe from developing nations has bedeviled Europe long before the creation of the E.U.

Europe, "not as friends" but "to conquer, and they will conquer by populating Europe" with their children. "Victory will come to us from the wombs of our women." Forty years later, Turkish President Recep Tayyip Erdoğan similarly told Muslim women in Europe, "Have not just three but five children. You are the future of Europe." This tactic, called *hijrah* after Mohammed's migration to Medina in 622 A.D. – along with the spread of sharia courts distinct from national judiciaries, and the belief among jihadist theorists that welfare transfers constitute *jizya*, the divinely sanctioned payments infidels owe to Muslims – shows that for modern jihadists, Europe's destiny is to become Islamic by infiltration and piecemeal Islamization, as well as by demoralizing terrorist attacks.

The flow of Middle Eastern migrants has abated for now, but the problems of immigration persist. German security services are projecting a new mass influx of migrants in the last months of 2017, using the supposedly closed Balkan route. And more migrants are coming from jihadist-infested Libya – 97,000 have reached Italy, the point of entry for Mediterranean countries, so far just this year. New migration routes are developing from Morocco to Spain, providing safer access for the families of migrants already in Europe. Continued migration means that Eurosceptic political parties – thought to have been tamed by the recent rejection of anti-immigrant populist parties in Austria, France, Germany, and the Netherlands – may revive with this latest influx and all the costs and social disruptions that follow. And despite recent polls showing that a majority of Europeans approve of the E.U. and its management of the economy, two-thirds disapprove of its handling of the migrant crisis, nearly three-quarters prefer that their own countries set immigration policies, and 59% believe that letting in more refugees will increase terrorism.

The current relief over the electoral rejection of anti-immigrant parties, and a seeming renewed faith in the E.U., suggest to its champions that perhaps it has weathered the nationalist forces that resulted in the Brexit vote. But continued migration, particularly from Muslim countries, and more terrorist attacks from self-radicalized jihadists or migrant sleeper cells, could end the honeymoon. More countries may demand referenda on remaining in the E.U., and populist-nationalist parties may see their fortunes change. The challenges to the "undivided and indivisible union" are not likely to go away.

The E.U.'s Fatal Flaw

The problems outlined above are merely the symptoms of the flawed ideas that lie behind the whole E.U. project. The dream of European unification embodied in the E.U. is based on the assumption that nationalism is a premodern relic and dangerously irrational. The evils wrought by Nazism's and fascism's "blood and soil" ethno-nationalism supposedly proved that exclusionary national identities hinder what for nearly two centuries has been the dream of the West: All humans share not just the potential, but an innate preference for the same Western goods such as leisure, affluence, individual rights, freedom, and peaceful coexistence. And since all humans are "plastic," they can, with the right social-political order, be shaped and improved in order to achieve Western ideals like human rights, confessional tolerance, sex equality, and political freedom. The result of such transnational government would be a global order enjoying prosperity, social justice, and "perpetual peace," as Immanuel Kant's influential 1795 essay was titled. Only the irrational passions of nationalist bitter-enders and backward people of faith are preventing the realization of this ideal.

Thus the sovereign European nation-states should cede much of their authority to the E.U.: a transnational, secular institution staffed by technocrats who will achieve peace and prosperity by practicing what French political philosopher Chantal Delsol calls "techno-politics," a mode of governing through rational techniques and policies wielded by "experts" working in government agencies and bureaus. Such a technocracy is superior to the irrational passions and exclusionary superstitions that lie behind a "blinkered nationalism," as Italian Prime Minister Paolo Gentiloni called it, and its parochial politics. This utopian antidemocratic vision was summarized in a March 2017 speech by E.U. Commission President Jean-Claude Juncker: "The future of Europe cannot be held hostage by electoral cycles, party politics or short-term wins … Brexit – however regrettable and painful it may be – will not be able to stop the EU on its march towards its future … Europe is more than markets, goods and money. The single market and the euro area are not ends in themselves. They have to serve man ... We cannot allow the people who defend these values – which I wish were universal – to be drowned out by loud nationalistic slogans which use patriotism as a weapon against others."

As French political philosopher Pierre Manent has argued, however, this characterization of nationalism and national identity is tendentious and ideologically skewed toward a naïve universalism and secular materialism. And it ignores how democracy came to the West in the first place. Modern democracy first arose in European nation-states as a way of uniting a particularly defined group of people into a "political community," as Manent writes, an identity that "joined the immemorial past with the indefinite future." Creating this "political community" was the achievement of the democratic nation-state: "The sovereign state and representative government are the two great artifices that have allowed us to accommodate huge masses of human beings within an order of civilization and liberty." This national community became the grounds of political "consent," the democratic institutions through which citizens participate in determining how their lives are run, their national identities expressed and protected, and collective aims pursued.

But today, Manent continues, "the state is less and less sovereign, and government is less and less representative," a condition obvious in the transnational, centralized, and intrusive E.U. bureaucracy and its coercive regulatory regime. The result is a "paralyzing disproportion between the weakness at the heart of our political communities and the enormity of their instruments." What is missing is the political meaning of democracy, "the self-government of a people," its place taken by "enlightened despotism," the "sum of agencies, administrations, courts of justice, and commissions that lay down the law – or, better, rules – for us more and more meticulously." That is, the E.U., which by demonizing all nationalisms because of the excesses of deformed ones like fascism and Nazism, has justified both the increasing concentration of power at the expense of democratic consent, and the marginalization of the particular identities of individual European states comprising various cultures, mores, religions, traditions, histories, and folkways.

Another important factor in weakening Europe's historical identities is the decline of faith in Christianity evident across Europe. The philosophical infrastructure of the West was built by the Christian faith, which synthesized the civilizations of Greece, Rome, and Jerusalem and created the goods we all prize: the separation of church and state, the importance of rationalism in human life, the value of the individual, equality, and "peace, freedom, democracy, human rights and the rule of law," as the E.U. bragged during the anniversary celebration in Rome. And it was in the name of Christ that Europeans battled for more than a millennium against the brutal invasions and occupations of their lands by the armies of Allah, a collective experience that helped solidify European identity.

Today, however, large numbers of Europeans, particularly the elites who have benefitted the most from the E.U.'s technocratic

---

The dream of European unification embodied in the E.U. is based on the assumption that nationalism is a premodern relic and dangerously irrational.

---

order, have forgotten God, and public culture has become "Christophobic." "Frequent" church attendance averages half the 60% reported for the U.S., and the numbers of Europeans who believe that "religion is very important in their lives" averages less than half the 53% of Americans who answer yes. Even in traditional Catholic countries like

Ireland, France, Poland, and Spain, church attendance has been steadily declining. In Oxford's *Public Opinion Quarterly* summary of global church attendance trends, only one of the 27 E.U. states, Romania, is not listed under "low and stable" or "declining." The number of self-identified Christians is declining as well. Between 2010 and 2015, according to Pew Research Center, in Europe Christian deaths outnumbered births by six million people. For European Muslims, who on average are six years younger than Europeans, births outnumbered deaths by 2.3 million. Unsurprisingly, then, many of Europe's famed churches and cathedrals are nearly empty on Sunday mornings, and tourists outnumber worshippers. And those who do attend are older and rural.

The decline of Christianity is reflected as well in the public culture and spaces of Europe, in which Islam seems to be the one faith allowed in the public square and protected by "hate speech" laws. The E.U. itself views faith, particularly Christianity, with suspicion, and views Christians as "shamans and witch doctors from savage tribes whom one humors until one can dress them in trousers and send them to school," as Polish poet Czesław Miłosz described arrogant secularism.

This dislike of faith was evident in the E.U.'s refusal to acknowledge Europe's Christian roots in the preamble to the European Constitution, a request some E.U. ministers characterized as a "huge mistake," "absurd," and a "joke." As Pope Benedict XVI said at the time, this refusal to acknowledge Europe's Christian foundations was "the expression of a consciousness that would like to see God eradicated once and for all from the public life of humanity and shut up in the subjective sphere of cultural residues from the past." Faith and its traditions represent too powerful a counterforce to the centralized authority of the E.U., which like all tyrants seeks to marginalize any other authority over the people than its own.

The result of the marginalizing of faith and patriotism has been a lack of any unifying identity and set of values, beliefs, principles, and collective goods to which all these unique, various national identities can assent. Thus people default to their traditional religious and national identities that are more representative of their daily lives and associations, a process that weakens the "closer union" of E.U. states. The only alternatives to faith and nation that the E.U. can offer are a "vague internationalism, a squalid materialism, and the promise of impossible Utopias," as Winston Churchill said in 1933 of England's self-loathing intellectuals.

In our day, we can add to the list the continuing attraction of socialism and redistributionist economies; a noble-savage multiculturalism that exalts non-Western cultures no matter how dysfunctional and illiberal, at the same time as Westerners practice a fashionable "unwarranted self-abasement" as Churchill called it in the same speech; and a *dolce vita* hedonism and "squalid materialism" that privilege present comfort and pleasure over the future of one's country – cultural pathologies evident in the failure to have children, the near disappearance of God from the public square, a flabby pacifism, and the suicidal appeasement of Muslim immigrants who despise the infidel West and seek its destruction.

The disquiet and discontent so evident in Europe today in part reflects the contempt and denigration of national identities and the Christian faith heaped on ordinary Europeans by the technocratic elites in Brussels and Strasbourg. But this arrogant assault on ordinary people's fundamental identity leaves them adrift. As French philosopher Alain Finkielkraut has written, "It is inhuman to define man by blood and soil but no less inhuman to leave him stumbling through life with the terrestrial foundations of his existence taken from him." With Christianity, the cultural and political foundation of Europe, a ghost of its former self, and with public displays of patriotism and pride in one's own culture and way of life restricted to athletic events like the World Cup, the Olympics, and the Tour de France, what today can unify the European peoples, or what else can provide the bonding solidarity of citizens, the affection for their fellows and shared way of life that motivates them to fight, kill, and die for their community?

The E.U. has no answer to these questions. No one will die for the E.U. flag, or a shorter work week, or a longer vacation, or afternoon adultery, or more porn on the Internet. And that lack of a unifying ideal worth dying for is why the Eurocrats have failed at their mission to create a united Europe whose economic power, cultural influence, and military resources would fulfill the boast of French president Jacques Chirac, who announced in 1995 after the collapse of the Soviet Union, "The bipolar world we have known is finished, and the world of tomorrow will be multipolar. One of these essential poles will be Europe."

On the contrary, Europe is fractured, its transnational idealism shopworn, and its very reason for existence limited to enhancing the power and serving the interests of bigger and richer member states and their economic and political elites. The recent reelection of Angela Merkel as Chancellor of Germany does not portend the reforms needed to unify Germany, bellwether of the E.U. And the surprising success of the AfD – nearly two million voters left the Christian Democratic Union coalition and three other leftist parties – suggests that Eurosceptic, nationalist political parties are still an important factor in European politics. The E.U., the government of Europe, is unlikely to survive in its current form, and at best will undergo reconfiguration into more culturally similar regional associations.

A Warning for America?

The American political order has for decades been undergoing a similar process of centralizing and concentrating power at the expense of the states' sovereignty and the citizens' autonomy. The result is a national debt approaching 100% of GDP, chronic bud-

> *Today large numbers of Europeans have forgotten God, and public culture has become "Christophobic."*

get deficits, entitlement programs approaching bankruptcy, and a regulatory regime clogging economic growth and intruding on private life and civil society. Birth rates are at 1.81, a historic low, population growth coming from immigration. The U.S. hosts eleven million illegal aliens, a low estimate, many of them sheltered by "sanctuary" cities embracing a naïve cosmopolitanism. And a self-loathing multiculturalism idealizes the non-Western "other," even as it demonizes the freest, most diverse culture in the world.

Though still more religious than Europe, Americans' Christian beliefs and faith have also been declining into a vague "spirituality," as progressives have been steadily silencing the voice and authority of religion in the public square – incidents of religious discrimination have increased 133% from 2011 to 2016. At the same time, they smear as "fascism" patriotism and national pride in American goodness and exceptionalism. Like the Eurocrats they admire, progressives prefer instead a vague "global" identity and multinational political order in which the U.S. cedes some of its national sovereignty to transnational institutions, checks its international arrogance, atones for its historical sins, and as then-Senator Barack Obama wrote in a 2007 *Foreign Affairs* article, participates in global affairs "in the spirit of a partner – a partner mindful of his own imperfections." No wonder Europeans still love him.

The improbable election of Donald J. Trump, who ran on the promise to "make America great again," so far has seemingly slowed down the program of Europeanizing America that progressives have pursued for decades. Trump's unabashed embrace of

The improbable election of Donald J. Trump so far has seemingly slowed down the program of Europeanizing America that progressives have pursued for decades.

patriotism and faith, pruning of the overweening regulatory state, reining in of federal agencies, restoration of controls on unfettered immigration, and appointment of an originalist to the Supreme Court are all hopeful signs that we can avoid the fate of Europe. And in Poland he delivered a full-throated celebration of the West that rebuked the flabby cultural relativism that typifies the E.U. and American progressive elites, and validates their appeasing policies toward Islamic jihad.

But like the sprawling government of the

E.U., the progressive "deep state" has burrowed deeply into the courts and government agencies, and along with their ideological allies in education, popular culture, and the media, are fighting to discredit Trump and block his policies. Progressive judges across the country have held back needed reforms in the vetting of immigrants despite the president's constitutional right to regulate immigration. Federal agency employees are subverting the president's policies from within with illegal leaks to the media. The media and universities are legitimizing a "resistance" movement that ignores or even justifies the violence of groups like Antifa against conservative speakers and demonstrations. Even in the sports world, NFL millionaire athletes are kneeling during the national anthem, disrespecting the flag to protest alleged persistent white racism. And a divisive, illiberal identity politics continues to pit Americans against one another, corroding the national solidarity vital for our security and interests.

The battle to restore America's unique character, political freedom, and national goodness — and to reject the model of the E.U.'s failing utopia — has just begun.

© 2017 by Bruce S. Thornton

All rights reserved. No part of this publication may be reproduced, stored in a retrieval system, or transmitted, in any form or by any means, electronic, mechanical, photocopying, recording, or otherwise, without the prior written permission of Encounter Books, 900 Broadway, Suite 601, New York, New York, 10003.

First American edition published in 2017 by Encounter Books, an activity of Encounter for Culture and Education, Inc., a nonprofit, tax exempt corporation.
Encounter Books website address: www.encounterbooks.com

Manufactured in the United States and printed on acid-free paper. The paper used in this publication meets the minimum requirements of ANSI/NISO z39.48–1992 (R 1997) (*Permanence of Paper*).

A version of this broadside was previously published with the David Horowitz Freedom Center.

FIRST AMERICAN EDITION

LIBRARY OF CONGRESS
CATALOGING-IN-PUBLICATION DATA
IS AVAILABLE

ISBN: 978-1-59403-999-7

EBOOK: 978-1-64177-000-2

10 9 8 7 6 5 4 3 2 1

SERIES DESIGN BY CARL W. SCARBROUGH